LIMERICK CITY LIBRARY

Phone: (061) 407510
Website: www.limerickcity.ie
Email: citylib@limerickcity.ie

The Granary,
Michael Street,
Limerick

**This book is issued subject to the Rules of this Library.
The Book must be returned not later than the last date stamped below.**

Class No. ......299.16...... Acc. No. ......C15900......

Date of Return	Date of Return	Date of Return	Date of Return
16 MAR 2011		21 JUN 2017	
23 SEP 2011		15 SEP 2017	
08 AUG 2012	15 MAR 2018		
21. JUL	19 NOV 2019		
14 DEC 2013			
13 JUN 2014			
17 SEP 2015			
15 NOV 2016			

Watch House Cross Community Library
Telephone: 061-457 726

ROB VANCE photographs Ireland with special focus
on its history, spirituality, identity and beliefs.
He has written and presented RTE's history series:
'The Island' and three series of 'Secret Sights'.
He has studied history and psychoanalysis and is an
associate member of the Irish Psychoanalytical
Association and the Royal Society of Antiquaries.

ACKNOWLEDGEMENTS

With special thanks to the staff at The O'Brien Press for
their patience and diligence and to Claudia Köhler of the
Medieval Education Centre for her many helpful suggestions
and ideas for the manuscript. Thanks also to Kevin McGilligan,
Jocelyn Vance and Beatrice-Brigid Vance for assisting
the photography with enthusiasm and practical help.

THE MAGIC OF

Pagan Ireland

ROB VANCE

THE O'BRIEN PRESS
DUBLIN

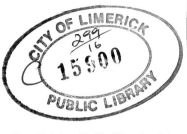

First published 2006 by The O'Brien Press Ltd,
20 Victoria Road, Rathgar, Dublin 6, Ireland.
Tel: +353 I 4923333; Fax: +353 I 4922777
E-mail: books@obrien.ie
Website: www.obrien.ie

ISBN-10: 0-86278-933-8
ISBN-13: 978-0-86278-933-6

Copyright for text and photographs © Rob Vance 2006
Copyright for editing, typesetting, design, layout
© The O'Brien Press Ltd

British Library Cataloguing-in-Publication Data
A catalogue reference for this book is available from the British Library

I 2 3 4 5 6 7 8 9 10
06 07 08 09 10 11

Typesetting, layout, editing, design: The O'Brien Press Ltd
Printed and bound in Poland. Produced by Polskabook.

CONTENTS

INTRODUCTION

Paganism is alive and well. It is growing in western societies and, unlike the established religions, is inclusive and non-dogmatic. It is a broad 'church' that includes pantheists and atheists, and respects nature and individuality, seeks expression through art and music and is not trying to convert the world. It uses imagination, the most powerful tool of humanity, to explore realms of thought and meaning, often on sites that have been revered for millennia.

Pagan Ireland is something we know little about, as it predates the recording of dates and events that we call history. But by exploring early sites or climbing the sacred hills, we may, through imagination, cross that immense span of time and capture a little of that pagan presence. When one is alone in these places, it is not difficult to hear, or rather sense something uncanny ... and wonder.

In the animated world of pagan Ireland, supernatural beings were everywhere and in everything. A sense of the sublime was important to those early people and many of their elaborate ceremonial structures remain, in varying degrees of preservation. Some are labyrinthine and claustrophobic, encircled and inscribed with mysterious symbols; others stand as proud phallic stones – cenotaphs, perhaps, to fallen warriors. These early monuments, mute, brutal almost, testify to a need to be remembered, to strike a chord in the void of space-time and be heard across the millennia. We are fortunate in Ireland that many still stand.

This book aims to introduce some of the pagan sites of Ireland, some of which are forgotten or unknown. Many are resonant with atmosphere, as if their undisturbed nature retains a little of what went before. Arguably, visiting ancient pagan sites is unsettling, disturbing to our modern ego, as if something primitive remains, a vestige of ancient primal life, awaiting ignition through contact.

So this book is first and foremost an experiential guide for those who wish to walk the soil of pagan Ireland and experience the sites for themselves. It is for those who seek the goddess and her consorts in the underworld beneath the graves of kings, where shamans withstood the terror.

Many sites in this book are overgrown, standing guard

over ancient roadways that first saw the chariots of kings and warriors perhaps seventeen hundred years ago. Other sites are named after goddesses and carry their presence in form and quietude. Some are truly eerie.

If you wish to experience these sites, I suggest that you don't go at night, or under intoxication or artificial stimulation. It may be best to visit with a friend who can assist you if you feel unwell or anxious, as the subjective atmosphere at some tombs and sites may trigger unsettling and disturbing reactions.

Many places are difficult to access and may require permission. Some can be physically dangerous, because of rocks, branches or steep hills. Pagan Ireland will test your physical and mental faculties.

GODDESS SITES

f nature was a powerful force in pagan life, it was also a named goddess, a personal female deity capable of responding to appeals with force or favour. Nature, as female, was like an unwritten ideology, a primal ether that sustained the tribe, a maternal body upon which they lived. Goddesses – nature personified – play a major role in pagan Ireland and in the Lebor Gabala Erenn, the book of the taking of Ireland, three women, named as Eriu, Banba and Fodla, beg of the invaders (Celts) that their names be imposed on the land: the name 'Ireland' is, indeed, derived from the goddess Eriu.

And if nature was perceived to be maternal, woman as human being was a bounty, the living embodiment of the deity. In her primary role, woman provided children to replenish

the tribe, and, as a group over centuries, it was she too who also most probably developed pottery, weaving, horticulture and basic medicine. She embodied nature – and nature, in turn, was her reflection. The hills were named after woman, the streams and rivers were her gift and at death tribal people of note were returned to the shadows of a stone womb.

PAPS OF ANU, CO. KERRY

The Paps of Anu are the most sacred mountains in the south-west of Ireland. These breast-like peaks, complete with nipple-like cairns on their summits, rise gracefully from the surrounding countryside and are named after Anu, the mother goddess of the Tuatha dé Danann. Early pagan peoples must have imbued them with supernatural powers as offerings of valuable objects were deposited near the peaks as part of a ritualised landscape. Huts located on the lower slopes may have been the dwellings of guardians of this landscape or accommodation for pilgrims to the holy mountains of the goddess.

FOURKNOCKS, CO. MEATH

This passage-grave is one of a series of tombs that may have belonged to a dominant pagan dynasty that controlled the high ground where Naul and Garristown are today. The tomb is a circular mound with an unusually large central chamber and many lozenge-shaped rock carvings. These carvings, similar to other art of the Neolithic age, may have been of a religious nature, or may replicate motions of the moon or other celestial bodies. The remains of over twenty-eight individuals were found inside the tomb and it was possibly the family burial place for a

dominant tribal grouping.

Most remarkable, however, is the goddess figure carved in stone inside the chamber. It has a benign and perhaps maternal appearance, a cheerful welcome for the spirits of the dead whose cremated ashes were laid within. As the tomb has been dated to 2300 BC, this is possibly the earliest representation of a female deity in Ireland.

SLIABH NA CAILLIGHE, CO. MEATH

This is a huge site with a significant presence, dating to before 2500 BC. There are thirty passage-tombs here, scattered across three hills. A few have been excavated and have

been found to follow a rough cruciform shape, with strong, graphic engravings on some of the stones. There is no doubt this was an important site, representing burial site, observatory and ritual place. It must have been chosen for its proximity to the sky and its visibility above the early farming community. A large stone basin found here was probably used for rituals inside the tomb.

The sun enters the chamber of one of the cairns (cairn T) on the spring and autumn equinoxes and progresses diagonally from left to right across representations etched in stone. Here we are drawn to ponder the ancient connections between art and astronomy as the sun follows a 'pre-engraved' path across these massive stones. The sun

was, perhaps, seen as one of the most powerful deities, and its symbol, a disc with radiating lines, is a particular motif of megalithic art found at Loughcrew.

CREEVYKEEL, CO. SLIGO

This excavated burial mound is one of many tombs in Ireland that suggest the shape of a reclining woman, perhaps in the position of giving birth or receiving into her body the cremated bones of the dead or members of a cult. It belongs to a type of tomb known as a court tomb and is around five thousand years old.

Court tombs are also believed to have acted as 'temples' where rituals would have taken place in the forecourt. Their isolated position suggests that they may have been focal cult centres for a scattered population.

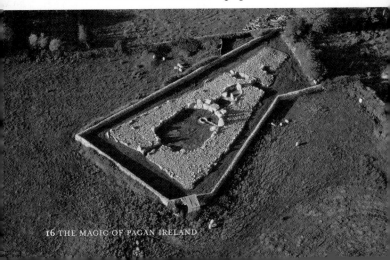

CITY OF THE DEAD, CARROWMORE, CO. SLIGO

This extraordinary site is the largest megalithic cemetery in Europe, and is overlooked by the massive cairn of Queen Maeve, legendary warrior queen of Connacht, on the summit of Knocknarea. Her unopened cairn overlooks this vast necropolis of over sixty-five tombs, from simple tripod dolmens to huge burial mounds containing secret internal chambers.

EMAIN MACHA, CO. ARMAGH

Named for the goddess Macha, this impressive earthwork, renowned in literature and legend, was, in early Celtic times, an otherworld place, the home of gods and goddesses, the capital of a powerful tribe. Macha, the goddess of the territory, promoted the cultivation of crops and acted as consort to the king.

The cairn that crowns the summit looks like a burial mound and was thought to be so until excavation revealed charred post-holes of an immense temple, 37.3m in diameter, with indications that a huge piece of timber, perhaps a ritual totem-pole 13m high, stood in the centre. After a century of use, the structure was deliberately filled with stone and burnt. Perhaps defeat in war, repeated crop

failure or plague may have precipitated the intentional destruction of the Ulaidh temple.

BOA ISLAND, CO. FERMANAGH

This long, narrow island is probably named after the war goddess of the Celts, Badhbh, who sometimes appeared as a carrion crow, notably on the shoulder of the warrior Cúchulainn after his death in single combat against his friend Ferdia at the end of the great Irish saga, the Táin.

The island contains a collection of idols, believed to be related to Badhbh and her cult. They stand in the small, atmospheric churchyard of Caldragh at the eastern end of the island, an eerie burial ground of an early Christian date, curiously without any church or suggestion of one. Their origin and dating, however, are a mystery. They exist as shadows within shadows, resembling, if indistinctly, the Byzantine-like figures that appear in the Christian manuscripts such as the Book of Kells, in hair, moustache and clothing.

Sites Related to Celtic Festivals

KNOCKAINEY, CO. LIMERICK

This graceful and rounded hill rises from a fertile plain south of Lough Gur. In the early centuries AD it was the centre of power of the tribal grouping Eoghanacht Áine Cliach, a subsidiary group of the ruling dynasty of Munster whose main citadel was the site of the Rock of Cashel.

Their goddess, Áine, had, in the tradition of Celtic goddesses, a complex nature, her character being interwoven with hunting prowess, fertility and death itself. She would have been their territorial focus and rulers would have sworn fealty to her, in order to ensure fertility of crops, animals and the tribe itself.

The hill lies behind the tiny hamlet of Knockainy, where people still remember their grandparents talking about ancient festivities that took place around the time of Bealtaine, 1 May, one of the great festivals of the Celtic annual cycle. Local people would walk around the hill at night carrying lighting embers in honour of Áine, 'The Bright One', and ask for her help in the fertility of crops and cattle.

TLACHTGA (THE HILL OF WARD), CO. MEATH

This high hill, named after the goddess Tlachtga, is surmounted by the concentric rings of a massive 149m diameter ringfort, possibly where human and animal victims of Crom, a bloodthirsty male god, were burnt.

The goddess Tlachtga may symbolise the overthrow of female gods. The story goes that she was sexually violated

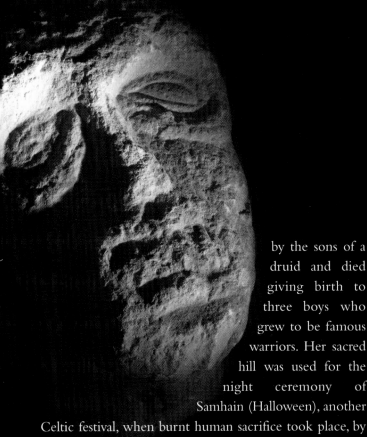

by the sons of a druid and died giving birth to three boys who grew to be famous warriors. Her sacred hill was used for the night ceremony of Samhain (Halloween), another Celtic festival, when burnt human sacrifice took place, by tradition, in a huge wicker man. This dark festival came at the onset of winter when the spirits of the otherworld emerged at certain places across Ireland.

OTHERWORLD
FEMALE SPIRITS

THE BANSHEE, MANY LOCATIONS

The eerie wail of the banshee, the female death messenger, is one of the oldest legends of Europe, and solitary banshees, warning of impending death, occur in the earliest Gaelic manuscripts, with Hiberno-Norman accounts dating from the Middle Ages. Perhaps she is an aural manifestation of the old territorial female gods, who at one time were closely associated with ruling families – the goddess returning at the death of her followers. The banshee is very often associated with particular places or sites, such as rocks.

In Wexford town, for example, she is said to be heard

around Cromwell's Fort and near a huge cleft rock at the bottom of Bernadette Place, near 'the Faythe', the medieval part of the town. She is described as 'wearing a grey cloak over a green dress' and having 'red eyes from continually weeping'.

In Glandore, in County Cork, there is a rock called Carraigcliodhna, ('Cliona's Rock') where the local banshee, Cliona, is said to sit. She is said to have lost her mortal life while sleeping on the beach awaiting her husband's return. She was drowned by a giant wave, the 'Tonn Chliona' and at certain times the caverns under the cliffs of Glandore are believed to utter a melancholy roar, mourning her death. Cliona is the primary banshee of this area and she wails for the Old Irish and Hiberno-Norman families when the head of the household is about to die.

LEABA NA CAILLIGHE, CO. CORK

This 14m-long tomb of huge boulders may celebrate an otherworldly female presence from over four thousand years ago. It was the dominant symbol in that ancient landscape and probably represented the claim to the surrounding land of whatever pagan tribe settled there.

When excavated in 1934, the tomb was found to contain, as a primary burial, the headless body of a woman; her head had been cut from her body and buried separately in the back chamber. This suggests that the bones were de-fleshed and then placed in a tomb – or something less benign. Either way, the site has a strong sense of presence.

KESHCORRAN, CO. SLIGO

Keshcorran caves are hidden on one side of Keshcorran Hill, where, in a legend similar to that of Romulus, a great and early king of Ireland, Cormac Mac Airt was nurtured by a she-wolf. The caves are accessible via a steep (220m) climb from the road and will test the endurance of the unfit.

The caves were possibly a ritual site, representing an entrance to the underworld and they feature in the ancient heroic stories of the Fianna, the heroic warriors of pre-Christian Ireland. In one story they were lured inside by cannibal hags only to be freed by a warrior, Goll Mac Morna. The caves are truly eerie and an archaeologist that I met on the site found a wolf tooth hidden on a high ledge, suggesting either animal remains or a cult necklace.

CEREMONIAL AND INAUGURATION SITES

S ome of the places where pagan communities held their ceremonies now appear only as undulations in a field, with little to suggest their former importance. But the power of these sites lies primarily in their ability to call up the imaginative space, to turn our 'inner eye' away from the techno-society of today towards the archaic and earthy world of Europe's pagan forbears.

DUN AENGUS, CO. GALWAY

Situated on the largest of the Aran islands, 15km from the Galway coast, this immense Bronze Age cliff-top citadel is surrounded on its landward side by a dense chevaux-de-frise, a configuration of stone uprights, apparently a

derivation of a sharpened timber anti-cavalry device first used by the Freisians against the Romans in 40 BC.

Legend suggests that it is a fortress, built by the Celtic Belgae tribe fleeing westward, perhaps from Caesar's legions in Britannia or Gaul. There appears to be a platform of some sort on the edge of the cliff and the ramparts too have a stadium-like aspect to their terracing and appear to focus on the 'stage', adjacent to the cliff, an ideal place for pagan ritual.

TARA, CO. MEATH

This hill is probably the best known and most famous of all pagan royal sites, traditionally regarded to have been the seat of the high kings of Ireland.

The summit has several ring forts and a Stone Age passage tomb, the Mound of the Hostages, the focal point of a pagan landscape whose monuments span about four thousand years. Lining up with the entrance to this mound is a partially hidden well, reputedly a cure for eye ailments and headaches.

Tara was the site for the triennial *feis*, a great national

assembly when laws were enacted and disputes settled. The Feis Temro, the 'Feast of Tara', can also be seen as a fertility rite – or even a symbolic wedding between the sacred king and the goddess Medb, symbolising the sovereignty of Tara. The feast was apparently last held by Diarmait Mac Cerbaill in AD 560, but then discarded as Christianity took over.

The Lia Fáil standing stone, a phallic pillar, was reputed to cry out when a future king rode his chariot around the magical stone in such a way as to cause the wheel hub to screech against the stone, thereby demonstrating his ability to control a war chariot.

DÚN AILINNE, CO. KILDARE

This hilltop fort of 40 hectares was an important site for the Kings of Leinster from the earliest times. Excavated in recent years, it was discovered to be a Celtic ritual site similar to Emain Macha, containing the remains of extraordinary timber structures.

Around the last centuries BC an oak structure of 40m in diameter was built. This was some type of circular stadium, with seating for spectators and an arena within for combatants. An iron sword and thousands of animal bones were found in pits on the site. It is easy to imagine some form of gladiatorial contest taking place within the walls over two thousand years ago.

Access to this important ritual site can be difficult and care should be taken to obtain permission from the surrounding farmers.

CRUACHAIN, CO. ROSCOMMON

Without doubt, Cruachain was a sacred and ritual site for the Connachta, the dominant pagan tribe west of the Shannon, and it remained important into the historical period. It was the residence of the legendary queen Maeve of Connacht, and is described in ancient stories as having 'halls' for visitors, being 'magnificent' and 'luxurious'.

This complex, extensive and mysterious site covers several hundred acres across townlands in Roscommon. It covers a time span of several thousand years, and includes neolithic burial mounds and standing stones. Its most outstanding features are the Rathcroghan Mound and several linear earthworks broadly converging towards the mound itself. It also has underground chambers used for ritual.

BEAGHMORE, CO. TYRONE

Lying on the edge of the remote Sperrin mountains, this site has more standing stones in a concentrated area than anywhere else in Ireland. Its name means 'Place of the Large Birches' and was probably the ritual and religious

centre for a large farming community during the Bronze Age. Around that time, there may have been a climatic decline, making it impossible to grow the crops required to feed the tribe.

This relatively unknown site was buried under peat for over four thousand years until it was accidentally discovered in the twentieth century. It is probably astronomical in purpose, although encouraging fertility may have been important also. A series of standing stones within the complex was found to be aligned to observe the rising moon and was dated to around 1640 BC.

CLOGHER, CO. TYRONE

This ancient pagan assembly place – burial site and medieval enclosure – stands on the southern intersection of two ancient trackways travelling across An Oghmagh, the 'sacred plain' that joins Tyrone and Fermanagh. It is

often obscured by early-morning mists that seem to bury the sounds of the twenty-first century. It is worth visiting at any time of the year.

In Clogher demesne are the remains of a ringfort, a burial mound and other earthworks, comprising what could be the seat of the Airghialla, the ruling tribal group of the area.

KNOCKASTHA (CNOC AISTE), CO. WESTMEATH

This hill appears out of the gentle undulations of Westmeath like a slice from another, more exotic place. Kestrels nest near

the burial ground and screech at the visitor if there are fledglings nearby. In early summer, its slopes reflect the pale green and gold of hay awaiting its first cut and in winter its sharp prow juts into the cold easterlies that bring sub-zero temperatures.

It was a sacred place from earliest times, and Bronze Age peoples of c.2000 BC chose this spot to bury princes and leaders. When excavated in 1932 the remains of over forty high-status individuals were discovered within the low burial mound on the apex of the hill, some buried with tusks of wild boar as a mark of distinction.

NEWGRANGE, CO. MEATH

The Boyne Valley was perhaps the most important cult centre in ancient Ireland and contains a series of three giant tombs and other ritual enclosures within the bend of the river Boyne at Oldbridge. Newgrange, the best-known of the three, played an important role in early Irish mythology as the home of the people of the goddess Danu, an otherworld race of supernatural beings. It is also traditionally seen as the house of the Dagda, the good god.

The building of Newgrange probably took up to thirty years and involved an immense community effort. It has one impressively large passage tomb, with four satellite tombs clustering around it, possibly for lesser dignitaries. It

is also unique in its alignment to the winter solstice, wherein the sun shines through a 'roof-box' illuminating the inner chamber, some 19m inside the tomb.

There has been a lot of speculation on the many purposes served by the burial chamber at Newgrange. Perhaps it functioned as a kind of philosophical device for estimating time and space by establishing a relation between the physical world and the motions of the sun and stars? It could, perhaps, have expressed the notions of past, present and future, related to the concepts of time and motion.

ARMAGH HILL, CO. ARMAGH

This site, where the Church of Ireland cathedral stands, was possibly part of the ritual landscape that includes nearby Emain Macha. Many early sites were associated with cult activity; these were religious sites where the deity was personified as a totem, which became the object of worship. They were places for ritual activity often conducted by druids. Druids could be women or men and they acted as intermediaries between the tribe and the world of gods and goddesses. They were the custodians of the inherited identity of the tribal group.

This mysterious stone idol was removed from a nearby rath in the last century and may be two thousand years old. The figure appears to clutch a wounded arm. He may be Nuada Airgetlam, (Nuada of the Silver Arm), one of the primal gods of Ireland.

This pudgy totem, perhaps an interface between humanity and a darker side of our nature, now sits with some enigmatic companions in the chapter room of the Anglican cathedral on Armagh hill.

MAGH ADAIR, CO. CLARE

This is the site of the inauguration of the Dal Cais clan to which the famous Brian Boru belonged. Magh Adair, disappointing in its current neglected state, is of great importance. In the past, the leaders of the clan were inaugurated on the central mound which forms the focal point for a complex series of earthworks.

The mound is encircled by a rampart which is higher than the mound on the eastern side and gives one the impression of a tiered viewing area, perhaps where the chieftain was brought to be 'inspected' by his peers and sub-chiefs.

Magh Adair may have been the burial mound of a Dalcassian ancestor, and the king elect would have stood on the summit while the laws of the clan were recited by

his hereditary brehon and his lengthy obligations read out.

This is a difficult site to find, but its state of decay retains a roughness and sense of authenticity.

TULLAHOGUE, CO. TYRONE

This was the inauguration site for the O'Neills (Uí Néill) and is a secluded and silent place. Its name means 'hillock of the young', denoting youth and virility. The site is near the O'Neill fortress of Dungannon and was itself the rath and dwelling place of the O'Hagan clan who inaugurated the O'Neills as princes of mid-Ulster by touching the incumbent on the shoulder with a hazel rod and presenting him with a shoe. Usually the king or chieftain would wear special clothes of silk with gold embroidery, or arrive on a special horse, all to become the property of the person who performed the inauguration.

Dolmens

Dolmens

Dolmens are among the earliest types of megalithic monuments in Ireland. The word dolmen comes from the old Breton language and means 'stone table', perhaps reflecting the belief that these monuments were once erected by giants or other supernatural beings. Excavations revealed, however, that dolmens were used mainly for burial purposes, but some archaeologists suggest that they were also ceremonial centres.

KNOCKEEN DOLMEN, CO. WATERFORD

This large four-thousand-year-old dolmen has an extensive

chamber beneath the two capstones and a small entrance on one side. This triangular hole at the base of the two side stones appears to have been deliberately created for access, perhaps allowing relatives to leave gifts for the dead or shamans to enter the chamber to commune with the supernatural. The chamber is charged with an unusual atmosphere, unsettling for the nervous.

GOWARD, CO. DOWN

This massive '*cloch mór*' or great stone is from c.2000 BC and its enormous 50-tonne capstone has shifted sideways due to weight. These stone structures may have had a function related to time, in that they would have established, in a hard and durable form, a sense of before, after and duration. This monument to the long-vanished tribe for whom it served as tomb and symbol stands in a silent grove of young sycamores.

STONE CIRCLES

Many stone circles are associated with burial and ritual, as little habitation evidence has been found in excavated examples. They are a retaining space, with circumference, entrance and focal point, allowing access to the ritual space within. Their circular form could also be connected with the worship of the rounded orb of the sun.

Stone circles are secretive yet open, sometimes with a hidden single burial at the centre, and, I would suggest, are completely different in concept to the chambered burial mounds of earlier times. Ritual now appears to be outdoor and communal. They do not have the gloomy and suffocating atmosphere of the earlier tombs, are not claustrophobic, and, even if roofed, are spacious structures, large enough for a group.

GRANGE, CO. LIMERICK

This large and rather eerie circle is impressive in its rough-hewn appearance and was a ritual site of importance for a pagan Bronze Age community around 2000 BC. The stones reach a height of 3m and the surrounding bank of earth is 6m wide in places, culminating with a 'representation' of the god Crom as a massive stone facing the entrance.

Grange and similar excavated circles contained human and animal bones and another circle nearby held, exclusively, the bones of children, but no evidence of intended burial. Crom was a dark and sinister being, the personification of darkness, and was probably the precursor of Satan in medieval thought.

THE PIPER'S STONES, CO. WICKLOW

This stone circle, with its standing exterior stone, lies on a heath at the SW end of the Wicklow mountains on the Baltinglass road. This was an important route to the ford across the river Slaney at Tullow, and the stone circle may have had some relevance to the community that used this

thoroughfare. It is noteworthy that several other circles can be found in this locality. The name 'The Piper's Stones' preserves the old legend of the piper and his dancers pirouetting in a circle: tradition maintains that they were turned into stone for having dared to entertain themselves so frivolously on a sacred day.

DROMBEG, CO. CORK

This fine circle is beautifully situated in gently rolling

countryside in West Cork. The seventeen stones are irregular and the primary stone is facing the entrance which is aligned toward the mid-winter solstice of 21 December. The place was probably used for seasonal hunting, although a curious gully runs from an altar-like stone near the eastern side, suggesting ritual and sacrifice.

The circle may have formed part of a hunting camp as a Fulacht Fiadh, or ancient cooking place, is situated beside the circle. These cooking sites could heat water to boiling point in 35 minutes using heated stones and were re-used over many seasons and perhaps generations.

CASTLERUDDERY STONE CIRCLE, CO. WICKLOW

This substantial circle has several massive recumbent stones, some over 3m x 4m in size. Like the great circle at Grange, Co. Limerick, Castleruddery has an enclosing earth bank, an east-facing entrance and portal stones. The stones have a certain masculine appearance – rough-hewn, arrogant perhaps, in their solidity.

BALLYNOE , CO. DOWN

This stone circle, 30m in diameter, surrounds a half-buried cairn, which contained two cremated burials when excavated in 1937. The site is approached by a long boreen (small cow-path) which meanders between tall hedges of yellow gorse and old field boundaries, suggesting frequent visitations over the centuries.

HOLED STONE, MEATH/LOUTH BORDER

This holed stone gave its name to the surrounding townland of Hurlstone and is difficult to find, hidden on the edge of a field bordering a small cul de sac. The stone is located at the foot of a large hilltop enclosure called Lismore Fort.

The ancient pagan rites associated with holed stones are still discernible in local folklore. Traditionally, they were sometimes used during engagement and wedding ceremonies and couples would hold hands through the perforation. Some of these monuments were believed to attract or ensure fertility and garments may have been passed through the hole to cure barreness. Other theories suggest the ritual insertion of a penis by arguing that most perforations occur on average 80cm from ground level.

RITUAL STONES

To pagan thinking, life and death were all part of the same matrix of spirit and energy. The high-spirited pagan imagination could leap across boundaries of time and space and produce art that was expressive and elaborate in its symbolism. While the important early tombs of Ireland have the greatest collection of these enigmatic symbols, later Celtic art was to turn earthwards as foliage and nature became motifs for expressing the artist's view of the world. Nature and the world of animals became a enriching source for spiritual and artistic expression.

TUROE STONE, CO. GALWAY

This stone originally stood in or near the rath of Feerwore in the vicinity of Knocknadala. It is decorated in a curvilinear style,

using chisels to cut away the material and leaving the design to stand proud. The stone was undoubtedly used for ritual and, considering that the design covers the entire surface, it is most likely that the audience sat on all sides, surrounding the stone.

Detailed studies of the stone show it to be 'insular La Tène' in design and composition. It may well be that stones such as Turoe formed the basis in style and form for the Irish high cross of later Christian Ireland, and it has been suggested that some of the Irish high crosses may have been pagan stones re-used in a Christian context.

CASTLESTRANGE STONE, CO. ROSCOMMON

This rounded boulder, approx. 90cm high, is one of a series of decorated stones dating to the Early Christian centuries. Its art style, showing stylised leaves and leaf-forms, is similar to the Turoe Stone of Galway, the Killycluggin Stone in Cavan and the Mullaghmast Stone of Kildare.

Little is known about the significance of these stones, but they probably were for ritual use, perhaps related to a particular place and tribe.

FORTS AND RAMPARTS

A t a time of warrior culture, tribes felt the need to build defensive forts and ramparts to prevent attacks or cattle theft. These walls and embankments are striking, though sometimes ground down by farming and ignorance. They can spark the imagination as we conjure up violent and bloody struggles that took place at such locations.

BAILEY PROMONTORY FORT, CO. DUBLIN

According to legend, this fort was occupied by King Creevan Nionaire, who was notorious for his predatory raids upon Britain, returning once with 'a golden chariot, a gem-laden chess-board, a cloak embroidered with precious stones and a conquering sword inlaid with serpents of gold'.

In an earlier period, it was reputedly the lair of a well-

known rustler and warrior, Atherne, who, as a ploy, kidnapped the wives and daughters of the local nobility as well as stealing hundreds of sheep and cattle. When warriors from the enraged families attacked his fort at the Bailey, Atherne retreated inside, while his allies from Ulster fought the Leinstermen for possession of the women.

DÚN DEALGAN, CO. LOUTH

According to legend, this wooded site is the birthplace of Cúchulainn, hero of the Red Branch Knights and a fierce warrior and lover of women. While he lived here, he was

known as Setanta, a name identical with the Setantii, a tribe known to have been in Lancashire in the second century AD. This imposing *dún* (fort) is surmounted by a Norman motte from the twelfth century.

GRIANÁN OF AILEACH, CO. DONEGAL

This stone fort may have been constructed by the O'Neills (Uí Néill) possibly in the Early Christian era. It may have been roofed and was certainly a royal residence

until the eleventh century, when it was systematically destroyed by the O'Briens in retaliation for the destruction of their chief seat at Kincora, Co. Clare. The fort is surrounded by concentric earthen rings and may originally have been a Bronze Age settlement. It sits on a hill overlooking the Swilly estuary and commands a prospect of several counties.

STAIGUE FORT, CO. KERRY

Staigue belongs to a group of over thirty large stone forts located along the Atlantic coast of Ireland. It is a wonder of ancient engineering. Its foundations are designed to 'flex' like a serpent and, after about sixteen hundred years of weather and depredation, the design still works. It was possibly a defended farm, but its presence suggests a more territorial approach to the land and sea approaches of the Kerry coast.

THE DORSEY (DOORS OF ULSTER), CO. ARMAGH

Some time around 150 BC, the pagan rulers of Emain Macha, capital of ancient Ulster, decided to construct a series of earthworks to prevent incursions from the south of the island. They relied on natural obstacles, such as lakes, rivers and woods, building their ramparts between these natural barricades.

The rampart is, in places, difficult to find, known only to farmers and archaeologists, but local folklore suggests that huge numbers of cattle were corralled within the Dorsey in ancient times, as quantities of cattle bones and skulls have been accidentally unearthed during land and bog reclamation.

The standing part of the Dorsey consists of a massive 6m-high rampart with a deep ditch on its southern side, enclosed by a high bulwark collapsed at both ends. This has formed a unique mini-ecosphere, filled with ferns of different emerald greens, with fluttering butterflies, and dragonflies, bluebells and bog myrtle, hidden from the world, perhaps since the days of this Great Wall of Ireland.

STANDING STONES

S tanding stones, together with stone circles, became a new form of monument in Ireland during the Bronze Age. Standing stones, powerful phallus-shaped pillars created by a patriarchal society, are thought to be markers of territory or important burials and can also be seen as sexual totems.

PUNCHESTOWN, CO. KILDARE

This standing stone, the second highest anywhere in Ireland and

Britain, is one of a series of three in the area, quite tall and slender, like spear-heads, tapering to around 3.5m. Their function is unknown, but probably relates to events or individuals of significance to their tribal grouping. They may have been boundary markers or indicators of where courageous warriors fell in battle, as a cist grave of 2000 BC was found beneath this example in the 1920s. The stone box-like grave contained the cremated remains of one male individual, buried with a stone archer's wrist guard.

If their shape and phallic appearance is relevant to their function, however, they may also have been a focal point for orgiastic activities at certain times of the year, as the Celts tended to procreate en-masse when the omens were appropriate.

CLOCHFEARMORE, CO. LOUTH

This fine example of a standing stone is reputed to be the spot where the mythological hero Cúchulainn died. He was the greatest of the Ulster warriors and his death, when he had tied himself to the pillar stone so that he could fight to the last, was in true mythological fashion. As he died, the goddess of death landed on his shoulder in the form of a hooded crow and his enemies knew he was no more.

The stone is on a slight prominence in a field and appears to be roughly carved into a phallic shape. It faces over rolling countryside and is certainly sited for maximum visibility.

STANDING STONE, CO. CARLOW

Two stones stand on this site and both have curious striations down their upper surfaces. These may be natural, but could also be crude representations of some aggressive weapon, suggesting that tribal groupings etched their 'weapon of choice' on territorial markers.

FAIRY TREES, MANY LOCATIONS

Of all the elements of paganism that survive, one of the most enduring is the continued attachment of belief to isolated thorn trees, usually hawthorn. By tradition, these trees are the abode of spirits and folklore has many examples of misfortune occurring to those who have dug up or damaged them. Many remain, a living embodiment of the beliefs and traditions of the past.

EPILOGUE

Paganism was to find a ruthless opponent in Christianity, a belief system gradually favoured by ruling elites across early Europe. This was a patriarchical religion, merging aspects of Judaism, the teachings of Jesus of Nazareth and Mediterranean mystery cults into the still formidable remains of the Roman empire. Paganism gradually disappeared. What did survive was folk medicine and places like holy wells, long associated with pagan deities, now conveniently Christianised.

If you wish for a deeper experience of pagan atmosphere and mood, the following may be of help. As I suggest in the companion volume to this book, *Celtic Spirituality*, choose a site that corresponds to what you need in your life – insight, courage or a wish to understand yourself, or indeed nature, in a deeper and more profound way. Choose a time that is perhaps less likely to clash with other visitors and, if you bring a companion, ask them to respect your wish to enjoy the site without radio, music or mobile phone. Leave the twenty-first century in the car.

When you walk upon an ancient pagan site, the ground is neither moral nor amoral. It may, however, carry with it a 'charge' like a battery, full of nature and the wild. Walk upon these sites, experience their primal freedom ... and enjoy.